CIVIL NOIR

◇◇◇◇◇◇◇◇◇◇◇◇

CIVIL NOIR

◇◇◇◇◇◇◇◇◇◇◇◇◇◇◇◇◇◇◇◇◇◇

MELANIE NEILSON

ROOF BOOKS • NEW YORK

Acknowledgements: Versions of some of these works were first published in *Pessimistic Labor, Writing, Motel, hole, Potes and Poets, Aerial,* and *Big Allis. Prop and Guide* was published as a chapbook by The Figures, 1991. Many thanks to the editors, the publishers, and the magazines.

Special thanks to Jessica Grim, Bruce Andrews, and James Sherry.

And "Those final Creatures,—who they are—
That, faithful to the close,"
Katherine Alford, Robert Johnson, Rebecca Quaytman, Brandt Junceau, and Jeff Preiss: love.

ISBN: 0937804-45-2
Library of Congress Catalog Card No.: 91-67073

Design by Susan Bee.

Cover: Flooded Area Between Memphis, Tennessee, and Forrest City, Arkansas, February 1937, Walker Evans. Courtesy of the Library of Congress.

Author photo by Jeff Preiss.

This book was made possible, in part, by grants from the New York State Council on the Arts, the National Endowment for the Arts, and other generous donors.

ROOF BOOKS
are published by
The Segue Foundation
303 East 8th Street
New York, New York 10009

for Mary Jane Neilson

CONTENTS

SPECIES OF FIT

my red room hangs there

Down the stairwell zillions of organs of adhesiveness, acrylic faceted stone questions zoom swore paint, feed reel the future, gate up sentimental petal allure, wild smelling runey licks. The way events cake nothing. Long muscular legs to prepare a frame for the reception out of patience out of space stretched toward the kitchen door confidential to the devil and the deep blue sea.

First a clockwise direction empty hand avenues of stones danced astronomical in abject curio array, time-lined blanks fidget horizon repetition. Letters worn backwards proportionately large, arranging me onward a variety of fits.

Torch setting rose cranny heat wave in a girl's face. Chief woe rickles, abandonment hives, shingles, actress pheric later a public measuring neuralgia: science registers the blush. Croon mysterion script depth perception sense heap—red went the room shades of the bus away from the plight driver.

blood count in the out of control tower
ultimate emblem
anti-depth
charge
if

Look out mountain—nothing to say to these stitched—nature gleam pit—the shaken nursery!—big zero tower—stormily neuron abhored—painted blind oration tilt these means—rock city—bed foot—come to herself—something flapped—sieve in time—switched coats in my head trails—hope it gets stuck in a socket shanty—face sweeping steps along—anemone humming clock—

Frightened at seeing life with a braid, monkey, bus, necklace, father, notebook, Fun House with deep public hex ends. El sueño being green the sensitives and looks my-her-then mouthed. Victualling lickkety domestic told dust spleen, honeysucking something utterly incorrigible. Dress hung on its side at the center footprinted blue curlew wrote soon my roots rain. Rote shadow reversal shamelessly piers, nose, pillow scarred to themselves think and stare. Thorny humming velvet beak cabbages into decades.

Singsong jasmine sweat in a greenhouse key, the fawn Bambi novelty planter swears light stripes. Exvoto vibe cube unveilable melon skull cymbidium flirtation rays walk possibilities, geodetic, affectionate inhabitants.

peel   owl
     tower scene
ear   pool

—screamed the geographer's birthplace—splotch head—it was a swimming-pool-shaped everything—err sir master specific—the little red cahoots is falling—shaking this chamber another voice in theory—grave violation—liberate shoulder to shoulder—plead millions loose—precautious silence—penetrating mirror

The perfect viewfinder twitch inside saying some days honey. About to be who goes there? Self-klepto between a raffle and red-blue sea megaphone trophy air waves aboard morale busting ebb-head. Misty helmet of anger, earthbound stars, all we wanted was our right to twinkle. Never-never nonchalance handshake.

18-in-1 minded anything *operator*, DILUTE! DILUTE! OK!
A Memphis grace period illuminating in its disguises, mist defy-

ing, spinning sexwheels, intestinal fortitude. People have to go home exceptions eternally. If not now when she-brick abc mason silencer and wrote it on the wall.

You with the bag, people have to go home. Yamboree head close the door. Terra del promesa California, Wales, Mexico house-licking finger-sitting dream-walking in the hole world. Information please—come closest ten years would off them, you know, the guy we met at the gunstore.

FILL   *jack*

a crock

jack   FILL

Disguised ten Junes why would *anyone* housesit them? Aimless spearmint stung minded desk hill top all scram humiliating spires appreciation lather. People on Sunday have to blood count brute home spinning copwheels get closed off coasthead operator hope yard (dog bowl). The whole gland splitting tears wood, cum grace, some whine, psychological bouncer construction. Lack willed a crock and lived to fall. Corner stores fuse—first shot I hear tonight. Debut, debut twenty-four plus stars.

This time shining on the sun. October mess tabloid dispose all bearing what's wrong betwixt latrine and federal scuzz trophies. What's wrong nanny, chervil lace wild spires traditional costume grit strapped in shocks the house. No worst, there is none. Peas mirage, hock water. Tracks pump the air newsprint herds long. Niacin flushed threshold the neck up from the mouth hurricane, vintage shriek strategy. End the distance and darkness in lost and waves the by away borne soon was she.

Precipice yawn the mountains of this remedial collision. Little pea-chicks kill stripped vine loaded with general opprobrium, show singing, a spring fire, the furnished slaughterhouse acidic planet.

singing, a spring fire, the furnished slaughterhouse acidic planet. Unless fox hair, ant cabbage, sunsetting grape lisp bird spasm. Lip coals burning rant drapery.

Not exactly smelling the roses demask tabernacle. Sign of the bleakest moments now exactly livid red leaflets darning prize-coming roots reign. Kitchen clock spitting chiclets. Often the hands museum of tantrum exhibitionist mutates unknowingly into itself snaking upward sweet lemon-gum showy tile walk. Popular new cacti garter marching bird night bath away. Nothing to say to these went the curio.

ITSELF A GREAT MAGNET

Souvenir girl brand attached to claim form.
Her scovery has drawn the thread
out of shift with thy gentilesse.
300---------200----------100
Color photo or Vegas strip.
Rebeck and warble me agri sous chef
a cleft canyon a wrong desert.
The pride of bath her Girl Brand water.
a 2000 seek to contour figure A-3
crochet U secretly tendering.
Heave small matter the while
a magnet can be used.
Of sugar, sand, iron and gold dust.
Intolerant skin but the other three
sham buss to cinch memory.
A rare device to apprize him
state that it center fetch.
Feet has bend page.
---pole star
U
U
U
---lodestone

---true north
I
I
I
---mutiny

QUANTA

Now then sitting on top of the world. Elusive flax as understanding commands. Fit the role to a table and see none of the tidal bone in four dimensions. Content to make a living these moments are based on the domino theory forming a landscape and maidservant who attends children. Could be the Garden of Fragrance for the Blind complete with discrete packets of energy as gratuity is public and equal. No other details on the tight-fitting scary toy but my one and only blares brassy at the wheel. Off the hat to end and topple if the first were knocked down. A futile activity in four directions.

ADIEU RIDES

Autograph my tangent of many-colored days. Detail from a 21st century tent anything but the point at which she breathes is a moisture trap. Privacy but not interesting. Soot comes. Because she does. A teratoid in chemise scores tenor then the supper club. Also teepee. Anything but the point at which she breathes. Land comes and does the handy pump dance. A cone-shaped bark in the night. This is a setback.

AFFECTING RESPIRATION

Better than is love.
A nervous sifting of rapid sea
some believe there are three toxins involved:
swimmable sequins through the blood stream
a panic sense or trace of argon
an old house filled with cracks.
This dance means fissure to you:
an old tree full of drawers
good distance in the customer
marinade draining fishless.
Believe don't come with patio
disappeared into Mexico
2,000 miles per hour
wind through the nervous section.
Breaking light and entering
two very elegant customers you know the kind
who keep changing their minds.
(A safe reliable source of energy)
shards mean they find you
or more nearly a fake walk through invaded shadows.
Distance means nothing to them this dance means
no thing belongs to us.
His funny archaic at sea
a presidential wink looming
sub-articulate on our horizon.

CLAIMS

"More people came and more people came.
Sometimes a single word or laboratory of sound.
Sometimes a short message when we return."

1. Pie Crust, Shaving, Fussing, Pending, Shredding
or Soldiers defeat season adjustment. What is a dead
horse when they are coming and they are going
and stopping.

2. A mismatch of imperfect steam shakes their dinner.
Consider the malevolent detective: his exact change
is different widths or inherent days of good
housekeeping.

3. Green clams know better and consider main land
tainted or other wise abused pets.

4. Maimed but yet verboten a vital air spill
with teeth to miss. Evacuation of institutions
on cinch turf.

5. Consider the climb as good as milk.
Our gold in seconds.

6. Note in her bouquet farmer at sunrise coined
from the peak, improper infestation. A lucky number.

7. All den bulge past and past tract chimp warns:
dinner should not be shipped or resolved to bent
orchids and religion, bread buttered by the devil.
Courtesy air craft and iron rot.

8. Imagine to be at the foot of a cultivated hill.
Coupons wilt here. Consider supper a hat with pins
to detonate when climb is neglected.

9. At the pond a kind of cannibal can drain dance
and sing mechanical returning early in training.

10. Beached cake is 10% duck and crinoline and complain-
ing.

CAPITOLA

Webbed feet teeter Western night border
freeze at winter in Friday hive motor
Happy driver stops for sight on road down
kindly opens window throws food to feather

Hundred eyes follow and footpad for auto
leave reeds faster break of night got to
Go one better table-bird over
ninny rider motions wing know close her

Swandown havoc gains bloom surround
grows lighter driver happy off to town
True ghost of outlast water blacks out
close bee noise honks teeter shout

Stars at border surmise green fowl
bubble wave vestments blow back hour
Eyes lulled open remember ninny rider
orange bills snapping winter hive motor

DISFIGURED TEXTS

...ught. ...

was fantastic ambition. mend.

people of this community, and named for you.

Hird sight to 20-20. Dis extremes

at it had better keep you off the streets.

Dull colorless plants and conditions exis
of all the surface feature, mountains o

s under the shadow of a larger figure. Your

mountains are the most common.

estrained and still eager to dominate. This

Three kinds of comprehension: literal, inter

ing out at an unshaken downtown, full of people

The coastal belt as follows — semi-col

memory or from the hillside vantage point of

Cryptic toward the equator. In fame

from the orchards and around the night

Great cities of the coastal belt heasi

akes, things we can do together. In trying

follows: Say dense vegetation alou

same time, try to remember I'm only a

A great distance in January with

she'll be coming around the mountai

To "pitch" means to throw, etc.

a shift in tone, is set aside for t

Lost in the words. urban provincial P

May I say as your elected official

Not likeliness. You cut off their heads
The coach has given special meaning

In a sweetish haze every action co

In a yellow wood, a sharp specific word.

genetic out shoulders as big as mine, an embrac

fit. called at death, sun, clou

Signed: a relaxed body, under drugs, loo

a concerned nurse. Cancer, disfigurem

your own size. These are cut down

coach. Acknowledgment and perfection.

by the herbicidal fog which blo...

words, urban prom...

Not likelicks. You cut off their heads
May I say as your elected officia...
The coach has given special meaning
In a swe[e]tish haze every action co...
In a yellow wood, a sharp specific word.
shoulders as big as mine, an embrac...
genetic outfit. Called at death, sun, cloud
Signed: ___ io a relaxed body, under drugs, look
a concerned nurse. Cancer, disfigureme
your own size. These are cut down:
Coach. Acknowledgement and perfectio
and perfect. by the herbicidal fog which blows in
The house, spots. Night spots like sweats or s
His dissaffection travel backwards and forwards at
with light and motion

Epigram: and the forest for the trees,
why do echos suddenly appear everytime
Intimations of an ECHO in the forest of
meaning but it fits. The sketch we
Why do birds suddenly appear, every
sleep and sing. How much can paper ta
to sort the thousands of headlamps
Comment your country. The tired
n[i]tion among the mass-produced cars
daunted feeling. A sun-clear grey
circled by an active avenue plowed
Do well doing good. Around a gre.
as a worker, laid-off from a produc
(_____) dying and b
dream work distinct from dream job
beginning. Adjoins said ditch. How big.
One ... heavy metal shapes wi...

Dream

24

... ... ~~clothes in a level~~ ~~...~~

here? Looking ~~for a~~ slip of ~~the~~ tongue and
solve my life.
the cheap visual frontispiece for their sex
on disfigurement or heavier than-air.
the handball courts ~~beneath murals of the~~
the most common. And yet no irrigation
endants. Some accepted expressions. A
is the first and last word of the text.
~~act in~~ the bungalows moves ~~towards~~ privacy

bed, hot ~~despite the~~ season, ~~sheets~~ ~~of~~
critical. The grand canyon. How green
umorously. I must have left it somewhere.
volcanic belt without no irrigation.
. about ancient art is on page .
han air. Intertinpunctuation as
. Decomposed surface features .
warning, ~~you're~~ sightseers in the narcotizing
othe. A sample of our words
sences, and find a full-scale embrace anyway.
re sex sez: "Handsight is 20-20.
temple saying "click," a surge from the
e had sharp specific word of what occurred
hirts ~~giving~~ up the ghost ~~block after block.~~
If they don't grow back. Barren mind.
to special words. an armful of some guru
~~edge~~ of reclamation. Playland ~~is~~ a space of
~~and~~ *Somambulant ambient text*
~~a name-tag on yarn left in the dirt).~~. Maybe
tip. One hundred times; and thou. Einsteins para
There was a steep hillside cut ~~back and~~
exercise and death; signed: a concerned
~~on~~ beam and stone bungalows were clustered on
score by Marcus to .

DISFIGURED TEXT #1 (Hindsight is 20-20)

Mend people of this community and named for you.
Hindsight is 20-20. Distexture it had better
keep you off the streets. Dull colorless plants
and conditions of the sure face feature, mountains
under the shadow of a larger figure. Your mountains are
the most common, restrained and still eager to dominate.
This three kinds of comprehension: literal, inferential,
out of an unshaken downtown full of people.
The coastal belt as follows semi-memory
hillside cryptic point toward the equator.
In fact from the orchards around night great cities
of the coastal belt heavier lakes, things we can do together.
In follows the same time say dense vegetation aloud
to remember I'm a great distance in January with coming
around the mountain. To pitch means to throw, etc.
A shift in tone is set aside for the lost in words.
Urban provincial may I say as your elected official
not like leeks. You cut their heads off.
The coach has given special meaning in a sweetish haze.
Every action in a yellow wood. A sharp specific word.
The horrible bug dying on the keyboard.
Genetic outfit the shoulders as big as mine,
an embrace called at death, sun, cloud signed. A relaxed body
under drugs. Look a concerned nurse. Cancer, disfigure, coach.
Acknowledgement and perfected
by the herbicidal fog which blow.

DISFIGURED TEXT #2

Presences to throw, etc.
Steve Sax sez: Hind is set aside for thur temple saying
click, urban provincial people had sharp spec.
Your elected official t-t-shirts up the or
off their heads and they don't grow special meanings shot
special words harp specific word. Sonam to death,
sun, cloud one hundred times.
There was a steep cancer disfigurement, exercise and death.
These are cut down I open beam and stone.
And perfection cidal fog which blows in with
pet horoscope hanging succulents,
remarked that I am dot dot dot spots like sweats or sits
of light and invisible ease in French.
Joy and envy awkwards and forwards at tear back to bed.
Light and motion was called out in for the trees
around the windows.
Appear everytime headlamps are pro cho in the forest
of trees quiet sonic ts (whole trees overgrown).
The switch we. The fingers much can paper take.
Thousands of headlamps a country.
The tired the mass produced cars
ate them through practice.
A sun clear active avenue plowed from as winter approached.
Around a great warmer climate laid-off from a product.
The park is lying and being in the minutes
instinct from dream job.
Vida loca, loose press my fingers.

DISFIGURED TEXT #3

Words, urban pro.
May I say as your elected official
not like leeks. You cut off their heads.
Of what shirts up the ghost.
The coach has given special meaning
in a sweetish haze every action bleak after bleak.
They don't grow back. Barren mind as armfuls of space.
Words of reclamation. A concerned word.
It was remarked that I the house spots.
Night spots or the house in French.
The playland a space of sonambulant ambient and thou.
There was a deep hillside cut of light
and invisibility. Places where the bed called out in the evening.
Trace forwards and backwards the forest in the tree.
Why those echos suddenly appear everytime intimations
of an e c h o in the meaning forest.
The switch we do when birds every sleep and sing.
How much can paper in the headlamps.
Comment your country. A clear sun prey doing
well around a worker.
The tired daunted feeling from the product lying
and distinct from the dream job beginning.
Adjoining said ditch. How heavy shapes dream metal pigs.

DISFIGURED TEXT #4

Intimations of an ECHO in the forest. Meaning:
cut, it fits. The switch why birds suddenly
ever sleep and sing. How much can paper sort
the thousands of head lamps the time.
The tired daunted country among produced.
Do well, circled by an active avenue plowed
doing good as a worker. Laid-off being distinct
from a dream beginning adjoining said ditch.
Impact dream-car you cannot be serious doing good.
The eardrum me you pine needle hoping vice roys, moths, nectar,
taillights waiting, follows you Andy.
And trucks standing by the park lake David just looks like
the canyons and riverbed. I situate myself isn't a plant
for certain enzymes (interference) or an oleander
opportunity verbage. Great distances in concentration
at night merge from the rest and have a 20-20 hindsight
distinct from the vain search.

DISFIGURED TEXT #5

Is park mending here looking distext off the streets?
Conditions on the handball courts, mountains are the
most common scendants. Your Mexico is the first and
last figure to dominate. Literal, inferential hot bed.
The critical town full of volcanic semi-information
ancient about night heavier than air.
Intuitive vegetation aloud the decomposed summer
I'm warning you're sights in January with moths,
with mountain presences, to throw etc.
Hind aside the temple Click the provincial people
and sharp elected t-shirts off their heads.
They don't grow special meaning to every action
specific words as mine. Embrace death, sun,
cloud one hundred times. Looksicle, a steep
open-beam perfection pet and stone exercise.

DISFIGURED TEXT #6

Here? Looking slip tongue solve my life.
The disfigured frontispiece for their air
the most common and yet no irrigation the last word.
The first and last hot season of the canyon how green
the tattoo. Humorously summoned as with the fingers
about ancient on the page than air.
Intuitive punctuation sightseer sez: a full scale
embrace is 20-20. SHARP SPECIFIC GHOSTS
don't grow back. Bare in mind Playland folk style
left in the dirt maybe one hundred times.
Einstein para exercises and thou signed
a concerned beam clustered by now.

DISFIGURED TEXT #7

Fingers positioned and hunt some siblings as winter approaches.
A warmer missing climate loose pressed the end among spirits
even you. After wings straighten out files,
what was the job left my friend's.
Try to laugh off from flower to flower
searching upside-down visitors in a dry park.
Jipped nouns in a good old fashioned spine-garden
and their angry algebra. Each path bigger or smaller
but wired with words to extrapolate as to peek.
And make us laugh at the normative conception
of the moths onto the next page.
The soul rules of thumb around a great silence.

DISFIGURED TEXT #8

The switch we I know the fingers suddenly appear
every particular sibling a thousand headlamps
unmarked paternal leger through practice.
The tired, mass-produced cars take the park
a sun clear prey, an active plowed avenue
as winter approached. Laid-off from a climate,
loca product, distinct from lying and being.
It off my finger, and ditch at you, how pig-headed
even among metal spirits car friend.
Now about the after wings shhh—take from flower
to eardrum. No way moths, or the Jessica lake
subjugated like algebra. I situate myself but is still
institutional or a mind to go on at night
with moths, on to 20-20 soul rules distinct
from search this great silence.

Note: Disfigured Texts 1-8 were generated from a composite of texts writ-
ten and exchanged in a writing, reading and discussion lab with Jessica
Grim, David Sternbach, Fiona Templeton, and Andy Levy. I am grateful
for their friendship and support.

SPARE TONGUE

Wondering around the meaning
of a necessity

so not the hours
but the proclamation of a bowl
circum digraph culents

uppish low words
terms of navigation
found full absence of feminine explosives

Fencing one lid
I relive myself

slot
spot
zone
turf
leeway
decay

Unknown (nature) various in various minds
perplexment enchanter
strength from strong

fround the word **sea**
unexemplified

TONGUEPAD

Accumulated in time by degrees
the fan not always the wind
great pests of speech

Admittedly bazoo optical spectra dress
(the notion) wild exhuberance
of ants ants in pants

Idioglossia will betray hesitation

drawled sort of humor
used to make
plum in one's mouth

haw care, breath-tied, voiceless

Or indefinite mutter clip by which
such talkee rattle means shoot
oneself in the hoarse

Rules as experience and observation
the uncontained

zipped cinct suck up

MOCK LAKE

Double cherry branch without
say Friday grasses and shade
in town fluency

Wreck cogged night wishing
some flagrant where
conversational
length from long

Some sources of the day: sky
wheeling in here interruptions

glass-eyed / yellow territory
an even chance cleft
sandal dugout / national homing device
ferocious reminiscence

And that is why reflections
themselves recollect
but cannot situate there

PEOPLE AND DISTANCES

The Following SESSIONS Being Weekly Accounts and Undercurents.

Bunches of daisies wrapped in newspaper bicycled over the afternoon. Spring softened, and washing how a lavender white and yellow Vacancy bombs. If what happened in the end had fallen in the water. The bend in a dummy's arm. Mind alarm extraction troubled awhile by visions. Mental swimming in the manner of a corpse found her walking. Now by plenty of time with a homeless aspect of the day. I cannot remain in the temple. Or I have a good friend.

The janatorial grit to work alone. I saw her through a space in the boughs. Diminutive plant offerings not a fixed map, as if a missile creaked, a tree filled, some body dropped prone from the condemned social order. Overhead a true propagandist that small lunch. Futurity on the face of soup. So a brunt is borne. And **auld lang syne** smiles out of every nook as if a strange fever of speculations and another sex were the exact opposite. I tell ya she's the same dame. Dare I say with scientific insight, a strong horizontal current of wind thundered offshore. **Un tipo suave.** Not a soul during that swoon bent head to meet it. A wall was not a wall with star jasmine. While drawing water, looking into the *tank* to see how the water whirled into the pipe and took the *dirt* with it.

Feeling touched but not subdued by the desire contained in this arrangement. For in truth, mama, you are the most unfading of evergreens and freshest of maps. In hindsight, it's always you. Smothered in stems. The industrial *strength* of this place and pitch blue outside present a different picture. Identical imprints of televised light and sound. Observe the paranormally yet correctly diagnosed siblings. Casketed with that first letter, the thorny daisy page covers white-pricked night. Can I have a raised look for this **hub cap of fortune?** The whole schmeer and speech of the thing?

One dark night asteroids and rocks didn't titter titter. With the instrument used by some to move the air and cool themselves: flame the cant word. Merrily mouthed, the body of the letter will soon follow. Cannot bare the bowl of roses washed down with vintage ink. Round on Sunday, square on weekdays: signed X the world. The patterns of extinction sweep me off your *feet*, wrestle anybody in the crowd for twenty five dollars. As it must for all stowaways, the moment of disembarkation arrives.

Working up from nothing to a state of extreme poverty. My ten steel pennies. A Federal post taste my reverie cue on the dance floor and suddenly something bewitching me. Ever more devoutly cold water on the piano. Just a voice set foot on one hundred bumpy miles of talking sidewalk. The dizzying height of press accounts. Still a long way to Earth. Beg the angel for twice as many genera. Time bought to pursue a juvenile duck-billed form and be done once and for all with dreams of biotic catastrophe. Assuming different meanings give the same word a place for sleep or rest. Lyric sampling the dinosaur food web musical: claws door / heal coal / telephone cold / a big chair / coat in session / chicken cup fried shadow / error bow / faints around the yard / head directly above eyebrows / my sin jar / look stamped / used by manicurist to shape fingernails. Venus is nailed.

This Thursday features fulfillment. From the moment I picked it up until the moment I put it down, all circuits were busy. Passing fish scents at Lucky Garden 12:07 PM and 52 degrees in a westerly wind. Three impossible news stands. American moving adventure. It is only human. Wet pant of hand-ironed shirts marching ahead of me. 125 lbs. and meeting people. The off hour waiting laughter viral mosaic. What can she do for your baby soft convention? What can you do for her gag-written fortress fantasy? More record-breaking weather.

Clay figures without arms overcome indifference when used by either sex. Great outpourings of lava during execution-style imagination rant. It hurts to look young again. It has been their habit to join bones together. The bloody awful country in simple vertical loom geometries. Trivial clannishness of racist unreadings. Fear of indigenous "communities" in the headless Navajo weaver diorama. Bring loose fists, palms toward each other, in front of body, at height of shoulders. Indicate the WATER, RIVER, LAKE, etc. Found Great Lakes represented by I SAW IT. PICKED IT UP. M. interpreted that although her visitor knew quite well that she only rented rooms, yet maintained in her mind and seemed fully convinced at that moment, that M. owned the house and would keep it. Further, that the house stood for her parents' house in "T", to which she was so attached, and to which she wanted to return, even by herself, should they, as they must, sell it.

(Lullaby)

The supposed lunar paraphrase pitch blue
To a mother of passenger security,
When, from landing to landing: soundless,
Hon(nora) a train traveling on the ocean;
Right leg run or left could leap
Parachute secrecy and railway line,
Right leg leap or left in mid-projection.

Two or three stars quiet
Answers small city object
Slept to sleep, no there detail burial;
Eleven, ten, nine clouding northern—
The cool shadow drift and end-all partner
Hand in hand post hour, easily
To boot together over earthly.

Bad big job babies should come clean. Then he corrected himself and said, "I am happy." Still a vacant country at the bottom left-hand corner. Rival buses drove round and round beseiged by evil eyes. All the while a pencil travels over and over the railway line in the shape of the female body. The smaller circle was the nipple. Ammunition trade names from Latin words. Newspaper envy fixed a network of young women as clean as could be on a muddy field. One of those editorial incompletions he threw to stop the editorial incompletions he threw to stop the clock.

The sequoia draped actuary wears an expression of deployment, from shacks to suites sitting in a small room—the point, being every night the lobby camera choosing a person talking. Increased vulnerability rabbit teeth. Do you want the tops? Safety Orange entrance to our favorite bridge. What was the tough chew self-construction of one long admired *salade* farmer. Got another gosh fright boo greeting eulogy bitterly yours postcard on the machine Christmas Eve. (Would you think W. had anything to do with the preparation of that bomb, for instance?) Classed a sibilant fuse; a sort of compliment. A schmaltz for a schmaltz. A fool for an eye. The so-to-speak public utterance of presidential simplifications in apple/orange food stamp confusion. Never before has a First Lady given the star drop signal.

If she did plant it, what about all this writing? Meaning to interrupt devouring furniture and speeding bullets. A hock-shop yes to the burlesque glove peeling. Playing a one-armed bandit can have any initials engraved to pieces. Or expressing feelings to a Pepsi machine with my foot. You were saying something. There were nine or ten people in the class under a loud fan at five-thirty. Soon the team spirit discussion sounding out China massacre headlines and the front page photo arrangement of the dailies. Breaking down the names of world leaders brought us to the cafeteria break. What speak was that? The same gun and desperate bullets. Photograph of a person talking turkey. Remembering the sudden emotional reactions to UFO abduction accounts circulating on the coast. Humans in captivity, at the mercy of visitors from all over the galaxy expressing surprise and pleasure in letters to worried relatives.

Plastic goblets and candlelight stars of morbid decor, in the clutches of seasonless resuscitation. Bricked off greatness boasting the top fifth zoo in the country. Dinner is stewed, baked, or boiled in ashramic stillness. At hearth petrified logs lurch the real centerpiece of the room near the reinvested riverfront. Blinds me with expressions of employment. Must have the things you love, peanut butter, vodka, driver's license, pennies from heaven. Always a good sign the energy to clear the desktop. Dashboards in a kid's dream with lots of glove compartments. Rows and the typewriter smack where the steering wheel will be. The same night I ate the tiny chocolate word processor Rebecca brought. Two or three calls made from the intersection of MacCombs and Featherbed. A true friend wasted words to shelter for a moment.

New York Cop Romance discloses a team secret about the dynamic systems of negligence and too often contrived commonplace. The impulse to run is irresistible. Or dance frozen in the orchard. Put down **ruts**. No body to kick for a house afire. Why it's fun to be terrified. Making believe sticky, greasy, sugary wonders or superhighway drenched miles. Dial tone superb. Outside was the place to be with life pressed against the window. Weary blues signed a concerned nurse. If it could talk what would it say? Ouch, ouch, ouch. Ouch.

Never mind the prior dick, be fabulous and ravishing. Doing much of the imagination work herself. Trying to remember Steve's tale of the somnambulist text at library closing time discovery episode. Insured against deep editing. But always the brusque intractable vigil of the daisy, what to do, what to do—my heart's a televised dancer. Was it "rushed twitches present themselves as the `heart' of the matter"? Regret her Bronxian division and obvious mad on us. Make like a man in the last row and sit up. Or stood in bed. And swept the motorcade off her face. Florida a particular moving adventure of thirteen Southern States. M. interpreted that the threat of an invasion was a great source of anxiety to F. He would try once more to get a room in a hotel and bite through the oranges.

Armed thought and action proposes its own displacement. Constantly re-released on its own recognizance. The object re-union sirening sea wavers in unison out a glass circle. The heartening shimmer of vulnerability and conflict. I fear the home team's lack of imaginative intensity. They called it **Just Pie.** And I want to thank her for two Emilys and a Charlotte. A long line of Janes. Because I'm doin it. I'm disowning it. Want to get it to get up and go? Childhood powers of entering and picking. Broken school yard awareness stems between me and this place. A person to person abstract. Cherished beaming feet to brain in the animal shade. My galloping ouija composition of contrary states giddy proof of **breath.** *Cherish Pity, lest you drive an angel from the door.*

The unconscious anxiety lest this play end in **disaster** goes side by side with "why wild?" Or missile cracked waves between palms. Not subdued but touched ever cliff-side. For in scientific hindsight the scrub-faced towhee light sound. **Chewink.** Another fever of speculation and presumption coming round the clock. Forget the window a habit with me. Getting to be relieved of the chance to do nothing. All my mathematically straight collars and raised eyebrow activity. Last I heard talking would do any good friend. Better yet, going through these days, pretty unsatisfactory at a distance but shining in the grass.

BEAUTIFUL PERTINENT TAMBOURINE SIDE

I. *Kindling*

Beehives quite differently   shaked

                  "sparking"

flamey persimmon   dudeen scorcht

               the way the beads read

aced hum-in   pasty spectra

                chandelier

autopsy turvey   downdraft

my building I

ignitable disc   lignin

everything tassel

coal toss   throat velocity

"crowning"

unsteady melt   wood behaves

bird of time

lily head   skittle

                          "air-tight"

let the credit   egg on

                   decomposition by fire

dusk smudge   colander blight

                          recrisis

grunion aloud   waft percent ore

                     ignition buzzard

II. *Course of the Smoke*

Mouth floor

       serve herself view

original target beat out

       smaze

two bodies brocade in a conduction

       riverish

sub-tropical brow wing

       on little red hot

spot foot set

       blemish grammar

argot shore by heart

       Atrek

enormous screen source

       variously yawed

cosines of multiple arcs

       au jus

the symbols issuing

      entertainer

star under table

      pail

do a sing snake

      federal retardant

sleep where

      demonstrated branching point

salmon checklist

      other people else

smooth breathing

      smolder

center stage

      plush statute trash

minutes

      life detector

behalf another

      foot out

PROP AND GUIDE

for my brother John

PROP AND GUIDE

Glittering close to its tale
shot through drippy peach separation
the nearness "a moment ago"
apertunist gap

So much thigh frill
under the eyelet
show some bed
under the respect
horn mooing distance

Case of the missing puff pastry
filled with savoury volcanics
voluptas cords
vaut heaven

Baste away garrulous knee fraught
locomotive gaze
deep up a stocking

SENSE AND RESOLUTION

Coo the Twenty-Four
contumacy cotta
pathless morn hoots
pink 'rageous corner

Keen you any lineament
such airing nosy festoon
matters of aerial lace
teary amplitude

Mimosa touched so droops
light slaw degree
where creatures meet
burst what garden or
subject the implying
too la la la la la la

TOOTH AND KNELL

Lichen boot shape
pass tongue over
2000 cross words
inferno booster

Swoon forward *f* root
martyrdom by the sea
reverse charisma my
a century of register
marmalade out
human planet

When walls are grey
understanding wince
stamped jaws enough
cruciverbalist niche
love imprint
cloud secluder

TINY ON A TRAP SEAT

sub-tropical horror
make it warmer
more afternoon
size 10 pulp
fret boutique
sweet trolley
it's blossom
outside circle pedia
vegetarian puppets
make it in moon purée
into a fig of joy

LEAPING THE CHASM

does as dearie slips
wall of fairy possum
photogenic historian
one-atom band
in women's clothing
stun Monday
prawn in the way
her realness
a pussle pour
nocturnette do

LOUNGE WRITING

Come to bat my dove
candelabra tools
something of love
can put up
ears live with
lozenge doll asleep

A kick out of you
foolish trains
snap to, come home
are the luckiest
fever in the world

Fleshiest version
chanticleer toon
hay there my
kumquat station

LIFT AND GALLOWS

Slow-breathing practice
means a Paris hat
"vanish" outskirts
big animal suspender
mega-hari eclipse

The patient a city
"spirits" megaphone
the critical list
scaffold vs. lips
emphasis on arranging
underwater, underground

Vibe-led dice yard
bewitched swallowers
thinking hat to collect
lockpick thin air
radio cross skull
claim the litte sequel

HEART CURRICULUM

Body of movie
for what ails
but the Light
first thought
sore as aviation

"Freeze" moving prize
curvaceous oath
out science alive
come crashing
insane belts

This curious cure
Niagaravates
best costume

DISTORTION no. 9

To "chill" secret suitability?
Shun motif (left cheek)
them that's lapsed
sweet buds derring-do
old fool, new fool, every
fool but true blue

For arms sake
x-ray muddy shade
french my long-stemmed dress
shad character to
private april over
all shacked down
all shacked down

SEATED WOMAN by seated woman

for Jean Foos

"Whatever you do, dearie,"
recuperate for Melodrama
bells at sunset
daylights out of me
Gish-like cyrillic factura
soft broken blossom focus

Where or *how*
meet and differ
Victorian dead-end tender
cruelty for cruelty's sake
at long last
lick and skip
the radiant tear close-up

MAZE RECANT

In a word plaid. This here warmth all wood can give.
Funny sleep in card deck futurity—all lustrous
intimations of radiance, said to lead.
Slupps of recognizance. My-my gradient traipse.
Southeast snowing all day and around fountains.
Love the way arm in arm on tv these things mean.
Into the fire, earthquake Mrs. Jones
one more time lapse, old dig, gouge, scrape anything.
So we talked with several per hour.
A toast to motivation.
Ever on to the blood count. Ten foot pole touch.
If fate means anything, viscera you alot.
Look into last petal minus the smelling salts.
Even precipitation of raining keys dream.
An entire ocean intended me. Silence. Rides not words.
This reason for a specific evening. In a gutter hint.
The teased brunette to her outsized audience:

"I remember you, you're the one who said I love you too.
A distant bell, when my life is through, and the angels
ask me to fill in the thrill, infer this look that night."

Bursts of furious activity, stars rain out of blue.
Recall what a cloud, remember too, eye chart descending.
Knot the hour. Still burn lilt of mean flowers about time.
About dreamt lucky air cut above the shoulders.
Social ghost ahead underlines visit sounds,
lit incense hour signal, lick all maze bravado.
These things mean instinctual heart noose—smiling plants.
Put down the proverbial sun, glob dissolving lang syne.
Push the curtain back with the sound of it.
Pleasant ash things with cherries table,

winged better tornado than ladder and thunder.
About wavey time in air, one million cycles per second
out door and windows. Breathing room suddenly last outskirt.
Rooming fears re-murmur ornate concentration patter,
hear pearls under water.

WHEELIE (SUTURE SELF)

1.

Her answer began "My saucy mauve, my compact,
my identification card—this taken for granted,
this made active." The allbang galaxy recipe in
sight, a pinching classical spiral effect, electro
cromag, an ultimate ism. Honey fairly drips from my
mental representation. History shaped bodies.
Sat next to which ghost? Madam, I am Adam. Madam.
He had an opportunity to be pushed around. Suited
to sit with back to the door. Thud, thud, thud, thud
of architecture toes-tail-teeth lurk, lurk, lurk
with some hope. Evidence and predictions in the air.

2.

Paid to anticipate unknown words, trade answers.
This weepie closes in on an ostrich head in sand.
Repetition compulsion made active, sorted intricacies.
Dependent on krazy-nail symmetry and own two feet as in
admission of fact-based accounts of people who have
risked their lives to save others. Elsewhere seedy
mall er arms er sportswear er plastic tray underwhirrr.
Grim specialties emerge. Daily intimate reflex code.
A girlhood gala in the head of the table.

3.

Dressed to the green "I"'s, a flowering
of memory. Plants coming in the mirror.
The wounded monster utters, "Musica, friend."
Away, lonesome sensation, away sensational tune.
No. I don't mean thinks, I mean feels.
She sat with it now in her lap, not looking at it,
only partly conscious that it was there. Only fruit
only feet only finger crawled across the birthday
cake. Masquerade handwriting will make a terrible
mistake. Elsewhere crazy mall symmetry shapes.
Hot rods, keyholes, skeletons found on eccentric
dismembered property, imaginary desktop.
It was not horror, it was covetousness.

PARAPHRASIA

The horoscopic promise of communication when kindness seems a trick

EVIL AT 11

"commerce is satanic"

1.

Accidents are golden.
Illness is believing
something in here besides
a language of symptoms
left to reader discretion.

2.

Hot talking their way
into a semi automatic
word blindness.
The way you love a tree,
ghoul spots on paper.

3.

The page world
pulls up a chair,
cheers up the pool,
feels the whole
series of household events.
Little horror faucet,
thumb swiped lamp base,
impaired bed time demon.

4.

The vocabulary of the average conspiracy kook
stops growing by the time he's 8 years old.

5.

"Chronic evictus ordinariness"
zoom to dot patterned
landscape on car radio.
Horns or tails.
Word dart/poison eye.
Pen haunt/ghoul sport.
Blank the goon.
What in hell is aphasia?

6.

Knee to tree for the umpteenth fang.
Come git bit
the hand that reads
one mean kitty.
Women, cats and cars
in the incidental silence.

7.

A hot-talking

slow walking

mohair god.

8.

Expensive pets rush to excellence.
Cheer blood letting in these beautiful digs.
1-800-TAPES dialed for a verbal advantage.

ODE TO HERSELF

"If that means am I gonna tie you up,
the answer's oui, oui."
                                    Brenda Starr

Where through the greedy fry
Does moral dementia die?
Buried in ease and sloth
From the perpetual waist up,
A state of emergency.
These role offerings, Comrade Mom,
It is the common moth
That eats wits and arts.

Half captive in tawdry finery
To be defaced by chattering pies;
See *offspring* possibly
A misprint for *offering*.
NO deduction or shelter
Allowed when giving an account
Of her life at fortune's pass;
Form of void rapport.

Carry on most provocatively in sleep,
The sensory channels glow false bait,
Exude numbers in a state
Of well known words.
The short term offered
Like a sisterly hand—
The handle of a tightly wound umbrella
The well-organized world again.

As hands endure reproof,
Arrange flowers, put back books,
The criminality of difference
And this slow progress.
A page to thrive people,
The memory funnel spinning aloof
But safe from security
As life already here.

(Variation after and with Ben Jonson)

PSYPSYCHO REMNANTS

1.

Reprehensible beauty present at the birth and death of stars.

The story of Cue.

How they come from behind.

From within the kewpie hole.

(Clipt yews grown wilde.)

Hi there my little vehicular.

My hydrophilic-serial-monogomist navigatrix
has stand-up do-nut up her sleeve.

A nice place to phallus.

Ruby ruby ruby will you rib eye.

"Why" at the end equals long *e*.

As in anecdotal embowelment pops like a car.

Or the salutary fluid of hello my little blow me.

Dex sex hex eye teeth.

Dorothy Malone father mamboed to death scene fantasy okay.

A tender chemical peeling.

You stepped out of a brain.

2.

The pasture is tense.

A made up country or state with flag invented.

Tell about the customs, describe the sleeping arrangement.

Tapping the conductor shoulder.

My fingers are snapping *me* and there's no stoppin em.

Frustrate miscellany aside; vile vial, vial vile.

Underground the great indoor scar conventions.

Handy candy. Seen but not heard the prelude to a cock.

Infantile freedom refusal.

Society and the Confection.

Society and great wet outdoors.

Society and red ruby caste subject in scarves.

Society and the working class fucking to death on tv.

Society clever and classless and free.

Data at the head of the table.

So home its labeled Casa.

3.

A house you can't enter,
let alone speak.

The reclining Boss Language as though what I meant was the
world.

As though two tongues had been stuffed into one mouth
making it difficult to eat, let alone speak.

The amount of money it takes to be hand to mouth.

Combing the obituaries for a singular experience.

A brilliant blue flower encaged.

Virtually orchestral against dark green grass parts.

In English something to eat, to drink, to rest on.

My stolen wallet to your car alarm.

Behave leafy with questions.

This quasi-legal repression practically the last thing on Earth.

Ants are good citizens.

The confusable arm on its own refused to be a wing.

Pull the "gloo" from the "i".

Spat on informers head by head.

I feel my liver turning cold and white like snow.

Dukes of Iron fight no bluff.

4.

A smut fest living in cities.

Excellent job, good social life and a terrific personality.

The best thing for you.

Unless the jaw is too small or the teeth are too large.

Go-go rhythm; what goes up must disco.

Metabolism check by any other name.

Good insects place group interests first.

The Prime Minister, shielding her eyes from the sun,
gazed at the races.

Prepared at least cerebrally for a defeat at home.

The repose neither earth nor hell can break.

But a science it is to suppose what illusion contains
(wish) we can't get elsewhere.

Singular sweat bread at the heart of the matter.

Now talking when unrecognized authority is in locomotion,
photographed darkly between sessions.

INCOGNITO EXPLODED ALPHABETICALLY

And so does a catfish begin to appear
because there was no element of submission in my voice, no
cinereal interest in flowers except as a dodge to jolly.
Discontinued style a two-bar, dark-field bevelled velvet,
flared arms, slacks off, curio suspension, roiling biceps
available in almond, furnishing sharp sights in darkness,
entertainment touch and go, pass the solitaire.
Digitally reversible into eternity bibiotherapy bio-as-say
fluctuant accident prone plot's worth of pianos,
every grand,
every professional upright,
every player,
every digital,
every concealed hood,
every previously owned waterfall seat,
every inner spring and contemporary shadow,
absolutely cineangiocardiographic hero-blasted.
Grisly thumb-print goes on telling fortunes
never exactly alike about a client to the grave,
never exactly alive the lines in the ball of the thumb
a future apparatus no disguise the dearest blood.
How to repeat the same old disappointed remark,
I trespass more statistics aloud the cost of funerals
jujitsu all the dislocated way home.
Kaleidoscopically fed back black and blue
lickerish and lucky enough to hand note,
that is, lie eternity prone between the brains.
Maintaining a reasonably unbroken flow of weather
both sides grew dainty in taste and memory.
Not obligate but roll arms, break mania together.
One night—it was towards the close of the war.
Presently presently panoramic a long glance
quark part of the city repeatedly the whole

stranger here itself always near.
Recognize me as bodily succeeded, never exactly alike
or too sick for arrest, but everyday a clue
taking things in order and dedicated somewhere.
Slight boiling all fours whole shoes surprising
the thumb's the only sure thing, no public
regulation exists to control it, doorwise.
Unbroken reflection as good as wandered
faces by the hour follow daylight exactly.

CIVIL NOIR

As matter: of particles I may as well come down
without another word (the dream a cinema deprived
of public, cordial mitral valved lying and being
you-ed atonement, she's too sliced for landing
to rare flowered bookie arms to can't talk now
her hands are dropping big lug spora to it was more
than Friday to o' the people with a black ball of fire
inside and outside a head maintaining the rhythm rhythm
of trade trade official culture soak to simultaneously
projected toughness and warmth, cynicism and sensitivity
and as for using eyes the incidental winking and blinking
animal watch me read seeing this the tone will glint
raunchy magnificence) but first please attention please
bring the demo room up to the front desk back up to this
fresh early place

DEAR TEACHING USING EYES:
GOOD TO SAY IF YOU CAN GET IT BUT NEVER PINT AT
WATERMILLIONS WHEN JOBS VANISH WHEN BLINDS JACK
SHUFFLING SLIDING OR TAPPED IN UNCONSCIOUS
IMITATION THEM CHORDS GRABBED JUST LIKE THAT
this nod to bougainvillea lit slantindicular playing
fork in the road backed up years to this day: airish.

MEANT AWHILE THE SAME SMALL TIME:
institutional augurates
power strapped little towness intestimony to thought
(towels for instance) prosaic with psychic gore,
patriotic fizz ed distress bed; re-input Ozzy Osbourne
about a million in the afternoon...

bye-bye love cocoa phenomenal
mighty recreation privilege
mightymightymighty calamity halo
mightymightymightymighty baroque love

(at the feet of teen preacho on the hillside
miraculous military pictograph coincidentally
scorned cells, portraits of the criminally familiar
in a naturalist frenzy of expectant sails,
clouds, foam, land, cold spit on raft
the flesh swept theme of disaster
one saliva bubble of spatial hysteria tinguished...
let me tell you about this place:

Text-ray emission: graveyard weather scene
from old fruit jar information and how
they keep secret house from so & so
                              Out to Here
...by the day...by the week... if this is a house...
the land it is on in a fency country sends no & no
letter but ploos of bare bones furniture lingual
creek counting "C-r-e-a-t-i-o-n!" thought I
better to tell a stranger (my peers, however,
are you made of?) CLIME UPSET TALL TELLING
read with difficulty the bored page is rage
spread thin as before and after *there*
the fustest with the mostest chattel indebted
plant mind hazard inauguration here ye's.

Down woo street of the actual city
      asphaltum
      up a storm
      shapely
      blue hour
      saw Veronica
      simism
      & darkness
      signature
      question mark
      the word
      in half
      shave & swallow
      solid thunder
      oddball
      atop no
      shadow
      deadly
      brisk.
      Eyesore
      coins left
      by tourists,
      petty genera
      soul chipping
      fountain
      of a replica,
      marquee tit
      eery
      (like a cake?)
      Aromatical
      mardi lyric
      into testimony
      shaft:
      se habla "injury".
      Trophy gaze

the primal smile
love & money
creeping
hurried lucky
crowd number
making up
genius guise
national
streetie
mistalkee
in a promo
tone enui?

"The—hiccup!—soul," replied the metaphysician, referring...

motorhead solo
bird counting
timeconsuming
solo
solo
outline
on the spot
might of real
a cult stirs.

mode of tale
code is sainted
marching intent
innards
network
department
of big blue
heart & bolts
thrown out herky.

the finger is
the finger
turned upside
down or reads
modestly declining
air—once—
papyrus hic-cup!
wall on foot
squeeze for tat.

third, third
degree fudge in
mixmaster
breathing spell:
hu! hu! hu!
he! he! he!
ha! ha! ha!
bon bon
aroused
shortstop...
inaudible gung ho
situation bright side
to razz clutch
freezes over a
fool's paradise.

the deuce continued:
being aged one year
and one month
so sultry swearing
most starve
the body affected
the body, the body—
wallet ballet
read leather
and a thousand
reasons parties
never experienced
a little rancid
agreement
parched
red
latter
a keener
epigram.

-ive story
out of the carcass
ifs ands or city
stiff harvest
puffy chin
quivered—
"it's hell
to die ugly
as this"
chafing
cookie
filth
pretending
nothing
chewed
match.

YES   NO

(clandestine)

Lo!

torched liquid ditty breast pocket floats straddled a chair
travellers now, bony, overturn length amazement, cloth reason
fiercely retouched (in the) numbing hoteled day frame

side of the discordant mouth spectacle abuzz glutton, a spy
for hideous curlicue doctrines reared very spent wheels
upped the discussion without a creek

neatly crossed hush takes glooms and shoe pocked time
five sights hard to pin

1 2 3 4 5 6 7 8 9 0
GOOD BYE

A residual feeling affected by wave action along
a body of water,

        defecation dreamt
        gloom bodice
        chintzy kind
        time cut
        very lip pact
        very bottled
        under Eiffel
        stabbed reader
        doubt learnt
        in sgool.

        Customary
        after soft arms
        to waist want
        jiggly smatter
        their triplicate
        stare nohow
        xia xia xia
        ginormous
        leapin dongs!
        who where to
        maskfully
        river trait?

Any irregularity
ammunition
for gossip
obsessional
honey flap
routine culprit
submitter unfixes
shade albeit
on a velvet hog.

However columnar
whinny her sentence
melted people meaning
doubt leans in
stop reading coal
access about it
by dog alone

leaves hallux
sill warm sill
subtitle afternoon
smear morning pan
cruller night curl
if only another
hammond couldhood.

Let it be misunderstood:

not comfort
but coloratura
fuzz box needer

not safety first
but souped up
innards in clover

not pursed prayer
carpet modesty
toy interpretation
white cavity
uttering space
only

Jot sir heavy
moonraked boxer
hope of southern
california

Stand, bow, kneel
noetic serenade

Moslem basketball
league knowallogy

Convert suite
on totem acquittal

not bough break
but bit
criminently
lip smacked.

Room filling chemistry
devoir civique

Ultra-ultra *this* in public
tongue bath

Black sopa de dialogue
cat slanger

Hardship draft
gong in one

Abstemious facial blade
sky pieced

Self of steam
purple brain

Bevelled idiom
wig cemetary

Fractures read
dead lettre

Onto molecular rivets cleansed fingertips out of the heat in a high strained valley, even thought white gloves a place out on paranoir this summer. Should somebody see sober hand shouts of light shot ragged blotto here-ville moving blobs very somebody seen history. Confidential and sweeping anything on me abstract hard lower lip genre neglect without children sudsy transition for the brief flashing record into mind squads smile a praise. Sentimental all toesy spells come of age starring an American. Latter day body intrigue thick beastly TV control beauties even. No I's on the blind side of houses watch the street after awhile frantic things shake loose hearty muttered guest of mouth I'll watch the house while you drink it hit a wall before we saw it. A series of the world smithy tire sing, fog smell, kelp rot, just try it shadows first noticed by French in the mirror with deep, distant eyes. The tearing sound tore it slowly time after time with her teeth the handkerchief came to tear it out and bit on it. As if to peer eyes open flick decanting the shine of them practically nothing visible even in darkness.

"Not if they sniffed him, miss."

Haw grave drawl something blinked line on the wealthy well grand a crack, everything on the red. Dictation dedication to and from inter (negative) memory indigo so Stanwyck fans out white earth. Enter (time) law of the golf course bravos grill breech drill melt socketry furious y más con stuck thunko, clubbed treeless aim, ate heroic steak, nice sore us genre, fat rink fingers running. Dear stranger or a rock to dilate upon. Blossom is bazoom swell hiddenness, born with "veils" over faces, etc. Toothy rattled eye more than accuracy I hear numbers flashing, smacked wave pseudo-dancing under the pretty strong blue dress, chéri. Coincident idea tefloned to pay hell alley iron word skillet helicopter leavings. Justifying mental cuts 'n scratches, it went everywhere, divided bandage debacle between loss and memory. Irreparable the incapacity? Now or then miraged much later symbolic barrier with a secret plan, virtually ocean with no one in charge.

"Simulated glory glory stain."

Scalded by the faith of ink a charging elk and lost it. Favorable but of course inconclusive private efforts a habit, combat, a canard portmanteau. A chair you should have brought with you here. Blandly personnel file the book, icebox, all. The article sounds bright instantaneous structural patter inside job gravitational. (Fig. 1. hat more or less meant.) Gabbled menu, meet hypergorge. Magneto-pause, the conky summer league. Notes on autobiographically reversed rear window plots: rumpled spectacles, broke shirt, smirking head falsie, shoe squirts, cold poke throws its voice bricks. Room filling chemistry ultra-ultra *this* in public: for want of a better habit, conjecture a handkerchief slowly dried the face continuing here. She just got a glass of water from the page. Part what goes over a fence last.

"The very ground hard as flint."